OUR LITTLE SISTERS COOKBOOK

CANDICE DANAE

FOOD PHOTOGRAPHER: MARI MONET

PHOTOGRAPHER : ALI SARDAR

RECIPE TABLE OF CONTENT

- PAGE 6 ABOUT ME
- PAGE 7 BUTTERMILK PANCAKES
- PAGE 9 CREAM CHEESE FILLED FRENCH TOAST
- PAGE 11 SKILLET HOME FRIES
- PAGE 13 VANILLA WAFFLE W/ FRIED LOBSTER TAILS
- PAGE 15 CHILI
- PAGE 17 CHICKEN NOODLE SOUP
- PAGE 19 SHRIMP EGG ROLLS
- PAGE 21 OVEN-BAKED BARBEQUE RIBS
- PAGE 23 CREAM CHEESE STUFFED CHICKEN
- PAGE 25 GRILLED SPICY PINEAPPLE AND SALMON KABOBS
- PAGE 27 PAN SEARED STEAK
- PAGE 29 MANGO HABANERO CHICKEN MEATBALLS OVER RICE
- PAGE 31 FRESH CUT FRIES W/ JALAPENO CHEESE
- PAGE 33 TERRIYAKI GRILLED CHICKEN
- PAGE 35 LEMON PEPPER HONEY GARLIC CHICKEN WINGS
- PAGE 37 PARMESAN CRUSTED SALMON
- PAGE 39 BUTTERMILK CRISPY FRIED CHICKEN
- PAGE 41 SHRIMP FRIED RICE
- PAGE 43 CHICKEN AND SHRIMP SKILLET W/ GARLIC MASHED POTATOES
- PAGE 47 CRAB STUFFED SHRIMP W/ LEMON GARLIC BUTTER
- PAGE 49 SIMPLE CRISPY BEER BATTERED FISH SANDWHICH
- PAGE 51 BUTTERY FOIL WRAPPED FISH W/ SPINACH
- PAGE 53 MEATBALL HOAGIE
- PAGE 55 HOMEMADE SHRIMP HIBACHI
- PAGE 57 CHICKEN BIRRIA TACOS
- PAGE 59 SPICY JAMAICAN BEEF PATTIES
- PAGE 61 GRILLED CHEDDAR-STUFFED JALAPENO BURGERS
- PAGE 63 SPICY COATED CHICKEN SANDWHICHS
- PAGE 65 (PUGGYS) PERSONAL SEAFOOD BAG W/ SPICY ONION SAUCE
- PAGE 67 ALFREDO TOPPED W/ SHRIMP

- PAGE 69 CREAMY SPAGHETTI BAKE
- PAGE 71 SHRIMP MAC
- PAGE 73 DEVILED EGGS
- PAGE 75 CANDIED YAMS
- PAGE 77 COLLARD AND KALE GREENS
- PAGE 79 POTATO SALAD
- PAGE 80 LASAGNA ROLL-UPS
- PAGE 81 CREAMY VEGETABLES PASTA
- PAGE 83 THE BEST MAC AND CHEESE RECIPE
- PAGE 85 TWICED BAKED POTATOES
- PAGE 87 BLACKEYE PEAS W/ CORNBREAD
- PAGE 89 GARLIC GREEN BEANS
- PAGE 91 POT ROAST
- PAGE 93 BROCCOLI CHEESE SOUP
- PAGE 95 EASY SWEET POTATO PIE
- PAGE 97 CRISPY FISH TACOS W/ SLAW
- PAGE 99 BLT SALAD
- PAGE 101 EASY PIEROGI
- PAGE 103 EASY PEPPER STEAK AND RICE
- PAGE 105 QUICK AND EASY CHICKEN POT PIE
- PAGE 107 SHRIMP SALAD
- PAGE 109 CREAMY SHRIMP SPINACH ARTICHOKE DIP
- PAGE 113 HAMBURGER STEAK AND GRAVY
- PAGE 115 SIMPLE TOMATO SOUP
- PAGE 117 FRIED SHRIMP W/ BUFFALO SAUCE
- PAGE 119 LAZY BEEF STROGANOFF
- PAGE 121 CHICKEN TIKKA MASALA
- ·PAGE 123 VANILLA CAKE CRUSTED CHERRY CHEESECAKE
- PAGE 125 TAN TAN MEN RAMEN
- PAGE 127 SPICY CREOLE JAMBALAYA
- PAGE 129 BEEF CHESSY SKILLET
- PAGE 131 STRAWBERRY CUPCAKES TOPPED W/ VANILLA FROSTING& FUNNEL CAKES
- PAGE 133 SALMON CAKES
- PAGE 134 STUFFED PEPPERS
- PAGE 135 SIMPLE CREAMY TOMATO PASTA
- PAGE 137 BAKED FISH W/ CILANTRO TOPPER
- PAGE 138 CREOLE SHRIMP ETOUFFEE
- PAGE 139 GENERAL TSO CHICKEN

ABOUT ME

Who am I?

I am Candice Danae, a content creator based in Atlanta, Georgia with content focus on food and creativity.

I was born and raised in the city of Pittsburgh, PA. I've went viral on TikTok for cooking food for my sister every day. Cooking has been something I've always enjoyed since the age of 8 years old.

What inspired me?

A lot of my supporters want to know what inspired me to cook every day. My inspiration comes from my grandmother Annette Thompson and my mother Candice Thompson. My grandmother has left me with some many of her recipes,
still to this day I have some her old recipes written down. Growing up I've watched my mother put so much love and enjoyment into cooking. My mother, Candice, has taught me so much,
I went from being her sous chef to being the main one in the kitchen. I've gotten most of my recipes by just being in the kitchen with mother, I am the reflection of her!

My experience with cooking?

Throughout the years, my experience with cooking has been such an exciting journey. I've went from cooking for friends and family to cook for hundreds of people. April 15th, 2019, I posted a picture of a plate I had cooked on Facebook. I've received so much love and support. It motivated me to keep going and catering events. People's reviews and support has brought me so much joy throughout my journey!

Who pushed me to share my ideas to the world?

Who pushed me to share my ideas? HMM... I can say this much, it started by my sister Mari Monet, the one who posted me on her account and reached over 10 million views in week. She has helped me grow our platforms from Facebook, YouTube, TikTok, and Instagram. The focus on our platforms is everyone loves how close we are and our bond, so a big thanks to my sister! My supporters are also a big part of pushing me to write this book. I've received so many messages and comments throughout the process of me writing. Believe it or not it has brought me so much motivation. The love and support are the reason I am in this position now! Candice Danae, myself has pushed me to share my ideas to the world. A few months back, I was told I could never write a cookbook on my own, which made me put myself up to the challenge. Throughout my journey I can say it was a challenge, but I did it!!

Buttermilk Cancakes

INGREDIENT:

2 cup flour
2 tsp baking powder
½ tsp baking soda
¼ cup sugar
½ tsp salt
1 tsp cinnamon
2 ¼ cup buttermilk
 2 eggs
3 tbs unsalted butter (melted)
1 tbs vanilla

DIRECTIONS:

- In a large bowl whisk together flour, baking powder, baking soda, salt, sugar, and cinnamon.
- In another bowl whisk together buttermilk, eggs, and vanilla. While whisking pour in melted butter.
- Gently combine wet ingredients and dry ingredients together. Tip: Stir in well but do not overly mix and leave some air bubbles!
- Heat skillet on low to medium heat with 2 tablespoons of butter and ¼ cup scoop of batter for each pancake. Flip pancakes over when bubbles appear and flip both sides until golden brown.
- Serve with your favorite toppings and syrup.

This recipe always brings up heart filling memories every time I make it. I always use to make this recipe for my dear friend, who I lost recently, Deondre L Stewart who was obsessed with this recipe!
!

Cream Cheese Filled French Toast

INGREDIENT:

French toast
4 eggs
1 cup heavy whipping cream
1 ½ teaspoon cinnamon
2 tsp vanilla
2 tbs brown sugar
10-12 sliced brioche bread
Oil- to drizzle
Filling
(8oz) cream cheese-room temp
½ cup powder sugar
2 tsp vanilla

DIRECTIONS:

- Start by making the filling. Mix cream cheese, powdered sugar, and vanilla until well blended. I recommended to use a hand mixer to mix the ingredients all together. Once the filling is blended, set aside.
- In another bowl, whisk together eggs, heavy whipping cream, cinnamon, vanilla, and brown sugar.
- Toast brioche bread.
- Spread a layer of cream filling on slice of brioche bread and place another on top like a sandwich.
- Dip sandwich in egg mixture on both sides.
- Melt butter and drizzle olive oil in a large skillet and cook for 5-6 minutes on each side on low to medium heat.
- Serve with your favorite fruits and syrup!

Skillet Home Fries

INGREDIENT:

2 medium size yellow potatoes(sliced)
4 tbs olive oil
1 ½ tsp creole seasoning
1 tsp garlic powder
1 tsp smoked paprika
1 bell pepper(sliced)
Half of onion(sliced)

DIRECTIONS:

- Heat olive oil in a large skillet on medium to high heat.
- Place potatoes in skillet. Add onions and bell peppers on top.
- Sprinkle seasonings.
- Lower heat to medium to low heat.
- Cover skillet with proper lid. Cook for about 5-8 minutes on both sides.
- Cook for another 10 minutes with skillet uncovered. Serve.

Vanilla Waffles W/ Fried Lobster Tails

INGREDIENT:

Waffles
2 cups all-purpose flour
3 tbs sugar
2 tsp baking powder
2 eggs
1 ½ cup milk
2/3 cup salted butter *(melted)*
1 ½ tsp vanilla extract

Fried lobster
4 lobster tails
vegetable frying oil
Dry Batter
1 1/2 cup red lobster fish fry
1 tsp creole seasoning
1 tsp lemon pepper
1 1/2 tsp garlic powder
Wet batter
1 egg
1/2 cup milk
1 tsp hot sauce

Syrup Mixture
4 tbs butter *(melted)*
1/2 cup maple syrup
1/4 tsp cayenne

DIRECTIONS:

VANILLA WAFFLES
- PREHEAT WAFFLE GRIDDLE.
- IN A SMALL BOWL COMBINE FLOUR, SUGAR, BAKING POWDER. SET ASIDE.
- IN ANOTHER BOWL MIX EGGS, MILK, MELTED BUTTER, AND VANILLA.
- POUR THE MILK MIXTURE INTO THE FLOUR MIXTURE. SPRAY GRIDDLE WITH COOKING SPRAY AND SCOOP BATTER ON WAFFLE GRIDDLE AND REPEAT.

FRIED LOBSTER
- 1PREHEAT FRYING OIL IN A LARGE POT.
- CUT THE LOBSTER TAIL DOWN THE MIDDLE USING KITCHEN SCISSORS AND PULLING UP THE LOBSTER MEAT UPWARDS. SET ASIDE.
- IN A LARGE BOWL COMBINE ALL DRY INGREDIENTS LISTED ABOVE.
- IN ANOTHER BOWL, COMBINE ALL WET INGREDIENTS LISTED ABOVE. MIX UNTIL WELL BLENDED.
- LIGHTLY SEASON LOBSTER TAIL WITH LEMON PEPPER.
- DIP LOBSTER TAILS IN FLOUR MIXTURE, THEN WET MIXTURE, AND THEN BACK INTO THE FLOUR.
- FRY FOR ABOUT 5 MINUTES OR UNTIL GOLDEN BROWN.

SYRUP
- IN A SMALL BOWL COMBINE ALL SYRUP INGREDIENTS LISTED ABOVE.

Chili

INGREDIENT:

1lb (85% lean 15% fat) ground beef
4 tbsp olive oil
1 tbs salt
1 jalapeno(chopped)
1 bell pepper(diced)
1 onion(diced)
2 tbs chili powder
1 tbs cumin
4 garlic cloves (minced)
1 (15.5 oz) can red kidney beans
1 (6 oz) can tomato paste
1 (8 oz) can tomato sauce
1 (14.5 oz) can diced tomatoes
2 cups beef broth
1 tbs sugar

DIRECTIONS:

- In a large pot, heat olive oil medium heat. Add ground beef and salt. Cook for 3 minutes, stir continuously.
- Add jalapenos, bell peppers, onion, chili powder and cumin. Stir until beef is fully browned.
- Stir in garlic for 3 minutes.
- Add diced tomatoes, tomato sauce, tomato paste, beef broth, kidney beans (drained and rinsed), and sugar on medium heat.
- Let chili simmer for 25-30 minutes after stirring occasionally remove from the heat. Let chili rest 5-8 minutes. Serve.

Chicken Noodle Soup

INGREDIENT:

4 chicken thighs
3 carrot sticks (chopped)
3 whole celery sticks (chopped)
1 whole onion (chopped)
2 cups of egg noodles (cooked and drained)
2 Bay leaves
2 ½ tbsp olive oil
1 tsp oregano
1 tsp salt
4 tbs butter
10 cups of water
2 ½ tbs olive oil
10 Bouillon cubes
5 whole tomatoes (optional)
½ tsp pepper
1 heaping tsp thyme

DIRECTIONS:

- In a large pot, add olive oil over medium heat. Add carrots and celery. Sauté until tender.
- Add onions, salt, oregano, thyme, and pepper. Cook for 3 min.
- Pour in water. Add bouillon cubes, chicken thighs, tomatoes, bay leaves, and ½ stick butter.
- Top it off with a lid and let broth simmer on low to medium heat for about 45 minutes.
- After 45 minutes add egg noodles and serve.

Shrimp Egg Rolls

INGREDIENT:

12 large shrimp(chopped)
4 cups cabbage (shredded)
3 green onions(chopped)
1 carrot stick (shredded)
4 tbsp olive oil (divided)
2 ½ tbs ginger

8 garlic cloves(minced)
1 tsp onion salt
1 tsp smoked paprika
2 tsp salt (divided)
Egg roll wrappers

DIRECTIONS:

- In a small pan on low heat add 2 tbsp olive oil. Add shrimp, ½ teaspoon salt, smoked paprika, and onion salt. Cook the shrimp for 2-3 minutes. Set aside once done.
- Place 2 tbsp olive oil in a medium size pan on low heat. Add cabbage and carrots. Stir occasionally for about 5 minutes.
- Add ginger, garlic cloves, green onions, and 1½ teaspoon salt. Stir in for another 2 minutes. Turn off heat and set aside to cool.
- Once cabbage and carrots are cool, add the shrimp to the mix.
- Wrap each egg roll (YouTube link below show how you properly wrap)
- Heat oil in fryer or pot. Fry 2-3 egg rolls at a time for about 5 minutes or until golden brown.
- (While frying keep turning until each side becomes golden brown.)
- Tip: Make sure the shrimp and vegetables are room temperature because the egg roll wrapper will rip apart easily.

Here is the YouTube link on how to properly wrap egg rolls. Link: https://youtu.be/yA5zTKw_gcs Fast forward video to 2:34

Oven-Baked Barbeque Ribs

INGREDIENT:

1 slab baby back pork ribs
½ tbs salt
1 tsp oregano
½ tbs garlic powder
½ tbs garlic herb
½ tbs lemon pepper
1 tsp cayenne pepper
1 tsp smoked paprika
½ cup brown sugar
Barbecue sauce
Olive oil-drizzle

DIRECTIONS:

- Rinse and pat dry baby back. Remove membrane.
- In a small bowl combine salt, oregano, garlic, garlic herb, lemon pepper, cayenne, and smoked paprika. Set aside.
- Drizzle olive oil on both sides of rib. Sprinkle and rub seasoning mix over the whole rack of ribs until fully coated. Then, rub in brown sugar (¼ cup for each side).
- Place ribs in refrigerator (covered) for 1 hour.
- Preheat oven 325 degrees Fahrenheit.
- Place ribs in oven for 2 hours.
- Remove ribs from the oven, and brush barbecue sauce on top. Increase the oven temperature to 400 degrees Fahrenheit for 10-15 minutes.
- Let ribs rest for about 10 minutes (to prevent from drying out).
- Enjoy and serve with your favorite side dishes.

Cream Cheese Stuffed Chicken

INGREDIENT:

4 chicken breasts
4 tsp garlic cloves (minced)
2 cups spinach(chopped)
2 tbs parmesan
4 tbs olive oil
Salt- to taste
Smoked paprika-to taste
Pepper-to taste
Garlic powder-to taste
8 oz cream cheese (softened)
½ cup mozzarella cheese (shredded)
toothpicks

DIRECTIONS:

- Preheat oven to 350 degrees Fahrenheit.
- In a small bowl start by making filling, mixing cream cheese, mozzarella, garlic cloves, parmesan, and spinach. (Using fork helps blend mix) Set aside.
- Lay chicken breast flat and cut a slit (cut a pocket for each breast). Drizzle olive oil evenly on each breast.
- Season the inside and outside of the breast with salt, smoked paprika, pepper, and garlic (SEASON BREAST HOW YOU LIKE).
- Stuff the chicken breast evenly (Divide the filling among the breast). Use toothpicks to seal the filling.
- Sear chicken for 3 minutes on each side on medium heat. Place breast in oven for about 20-25 minutes. Rest for about 5 minutes before serving.
- Serve with favorite sides.

Grilled Spicy Salmon & Pineapple Kabobs

INGREDIENT:

1 lb salmon filet, cut into cubes
(20 oz) can pineapple chucks
2 tbs soy sauce
2 tbs brown sugar(packed)
1 ½ tsp garlic powder
1 tsp cayenne pepper
2 tsp (salted) lemon pepper
1 tbs olive oil
Pack of Skewers
1 fresh pineapple (cored & cut into chunks)

DIRECTIONS:

- Soak skewers.
- In a large bowl, gently combine cubed salmon, lemon pepper, and olive oil. Set aside.
- In a blender, add can pineapple chunks, soy sauce, brown sugar, garlic powder, cayenne pepper. Pulse until blended.
- Pour pineapple mixture over the seasoned salmon. Marinate in the refrigerator for 1 hour.
- Skewer pineapple and salmon chunks until all are used. Place skewers on the grill cooking each side for 5 minutes or until salmon is fully cooked.
- (Ensure grill is clean and well oiled).

Cast Iron Pan-Seared Steak

INGREDIENT:

4 New York strip steaks 1-1 ½ inch thick
Salt – to taste
Pepper -to taste
4 tbs unsalted butter
5 fresh sprigs rosemary or thyme
4-6 garlic cloves -smashed
2 tbs olive oil

DIRECTIONS:

- Bring steak to room temperature (sit out for about 20 minutes).
- Rinse and pat dry steaks and season with salt and pepper on each side.
- Heat large cast iron pan on medium to high heat for about 5-10 minutes (or until you see light smoke).
- Add olive oil on cast iron. Place the steaks on cast iron and cook for 5 minutes on each side.
- Reduce heat to low heat, add butter, rosemary or thyme sprigs, and garlic.
- After about 1 minute allowing butter to melt, tilt the skillet and spoon butter over the steaks for about 20 seconds (with the rosemary and garlic).
- Remove the steaks from cast iron and let rest for 5-8 minutes. Serve.

Mango Habanero Chicken Meatballs Over Rice

INGREDIENT:

Meatballs
4 chicken breast cutlets
¾ cup panko breadcrumbs
1 tbs olive oil
1 tsp salt
½ tsp pepper
4 garlic cloves(minced)
1 egg
1 habanero pepper (finely chopped)

Sauce
4 cups chicken broth*(divided)*
2 mangoes *(peeled, sliced)*
2 tbs olive oil
2 habanero peppers *(finely chopped)*
2 green onions*(chopped)*
4 garlic cloves*(minced)*
4 tsp ginger
4 tbs brown sugar
1 tsp Worcestershire sauce
1 red bell *pepper (thinly sliced)*

DIRECTIONS:

Meatballs
- Preheat oven to 350 degrees.
- Place chicken in a blender. Pulse until chicken is well blended.
- In a large bowl, combine blended chicken, breadcrumbs, olive oil, garlic, habanero, egg, salt, and pepper.
- Shape mixture into about 10-12 meatballs.
- Using a sheet pan with parchment paper, place meatball about an inch apart.
- Bake meatballs for about 10-15 minutes.

Sauce
- In a saucepan, add 2 cups chicken broth and mango slices. Simmer for about 10 minutes on medium heat.
- Remove the chicken broth and mangoes from the pan into a blender and pulse until smooth. Set aside.
- In a saucepan heat olive oil. Add ginger, garlic, and habanero. Sauté for 1 minute.
- Add the other 2 cups chicken broth and mango blend. Simmer for about 3-5 minutes.
- Stir in bell peppers, brown sugar, and Worcestershire sauce. Simmer for another 5minutes on low heat.
- Add chicken meatballs and green onions. Simmer for another 5 minutes. Serve over sticky rice!

Fresh-Cut Fries W/ Jalapeno Cheese

INGREDIENT:

3 large russet potatoes-sliced
Oil-for frying
Cajun seasoning- to taste

Cheese Sauce
4 oz Velveeta cheese (cubed)
1 jalapeno- sliced
½ cup evaporated milk
1/8 tsp cayenne powder
½ tsp paprika
½ tsp hot sauce

DIRECTIONS:

- Slice potatoes into long slices.
- In a large bowl with cold water, soak potato slices for about an hour (the longer potatoes soak, the crisper).
- Rinse potato slices with cold water.
- Thoroughly, Pat dry with paper towel.
- Heat frying oil. Fry each batch for about 7 minutes or until golden brown.
- Remove from grease onto a paper towel. Immediately sprinkle with Cajun seasoning. Serve.

Cheese Sauce
- In a small skillet place in milk, Velveeta cubes and jalapenos.
- Whisk until smooth.
- Add seasonings and hot sauce.
- Whisk occasionally for about 1-2 minutes. (If the cheese start to get too thick gradually add more milk).

Grilled Teriyaki Chicken

INGREDIENT:

8 chicken thighs (bone-in)
2 cup soy sauce
2 cup ketchup
8 garlic cloves-minced
½ cup brown sugar
3 tsp cayenne

DIRECTIONS:

- In a large bowl combine soy sauce, ketchup, garlic, brown sugar, and cayenne. Mix. Pour mixture in a large freezer bag.
- Add chicken thighs.
- Marinate for 4-6 hours or overnight for more flavor.
- Place chicken thighs skin side up on the grill.
- Grill, covered, for 20-25 minutes or until is well crispy and done.
- Serve with your favorite side dishes.

Lemon Pepper Honey Garlic Chicken Wings

INGREDIENT:

Chicken
2 lb. chicken wings-cut
1 tbs olive oil
Lemon pepper – to taste

Glaze
¼ cup soy sauce
½ cup honey
1 tsp olive oil
1 tbs garlic (minced)
½ tsp cayenne
½ tsp smoked paprika

DIRECTIONS:

- Preheat oven to 350 degrees Fahrenheit.
- In a large bowl, add chicken and olive oil and season with lemon pepper. Evenly mix.
- Place chicken wings on a sheet pan.
- Bake for 30 minutes or until chicken is golden brown and crispy on each side
(Make sure you turn chicken during cook time to ensure both sides are crispy).
- In a small saucepan, combine soy sauce, honey, olive oil, garlic, cayenne, and paprika. Simmer for 5-6 minutes. Remove from heat and set aside.
- Once you remove chicken wings from oven drizzle the glaze immediately. Serve.

Parmesan Crusted Salmon

INGREDIENT:

1 lb salmon filet
Salt-to taste
½ cup mayonnaise
½ cup parmesan cheese
2 garlic cloves(minced)
2 tbs olive oil
½ tsp parsley (optional)

DIRECTIONS:

- Preheat oven to 350 degrees Fahrenheit.
- Lightly salt salmon on both sides.
- In a small mixing bowl, combine mayonnaise, parmesan, garlic, and parsley.
- Evenly spread mixture on top of salmon.
- Oil pan and place in oven for 20-25 minutes.

Buttermilk Crispy Fried Chicken

INGREDIENT:

3 lb chicken wings
(30 fl oz) coconut fry oil

Wet ingredients
2 ½ cup buttermilk
1 tsp paprika
1 garlic powder
½ tsp cayenne
1 tsp salt
1 tsp black pepper

Dry Ingredients
3 cups all-purpose flour
2 tsp baking powder
3 tsp smoked paprika
1 tsp salt
1 tsp garlic powder
1 tsp onion salt
1 tsp creole seasoning
1 tsp cayenne

DIRECTIONS:

- In a bowl, whisk together all wet ingredients. Add chicken wings. Refrigerate and marinate up to 4 hours (the longer you marinate the better!).
- Remove bowl from fridge and bring chicken wings to room temperature.
- Using a freezer bag, combine all dry ingredients.
- Fully coat each piece of chicken into dry mix.
- Place chicken wings on a rack and let chicken dry out for about 20 minutes before frying.
- Heat frying oil into a large frying pot. (Use enough oil to cover each chicken wing).
- When the oil is heated and ready fry 2-3 pieces each batch. Cook until chicken golden brown and crispy for about 8 minutes.
  Serve with your favorite side dishes.

Shrimp Fried Rice

INGREDIENT:

(7oz) yellow rice box (cooked and refrigerated overnight)
1/2 lb. large shrimp
2 garlic cloves(minced)
1 cup onion(diced)
1 cup broccoli
¼ cup carrot (chopped finely)
¼ cup celery (chopped finely)
2 green onions (chopped)
½ cup bell peppers (chopped)
4 tbs olive oil -divided
¼ cup water
1 tsp onion salt
3 tbs soy sauce

DIRECTIONS:

- In a large pan, place 2 tablespoon olive oil, water, broccoli, carrots, and celery. Boil until all vegetables are tender
- (And a little water is left in the pan still).
- Add onions, peppers, and garlic. Stir occasionally for about 3 minutes. Set aside.
- In another pan, on medium heat add olive oil, shrimp, yellow rice, and onion salt. Stir continuously until shrimp is fully cooked.
- Add in vegetable mixture in with the rice.
- Turn off heat. Stir in soy sauce and green onions. Serve.

Chicken and Shrimp W/ Garlic Mash Potatoes

INGREDIENT:

CHICKEN AND SHRIMP / GARLIC BUTTER
1 lb boneless chicken thighs
1 lb large shrimp
2 tsp smoked paprika
3 tsp brown sugar
½ tsp oregano
1 tsp salt
½ tsp black pepper
½ tsp chili powder
¼ tsp cayenne
½ garlic powder
½ tsp red crushed peppers
3 tbsp olive oil - divided
8 tbs unsalted butter
4 garlic cloves
1 tbsp lemon juice

GARLIC MASH POTATOES
6 red potatoes
1 stick salted butter(softened)
½ cup heavy whipping cream (room temp)
1 tsp salt
¼ tsp garlic powder

To Serve
Sauteed mushrooms
Sauteed onions

DIRECTIONS:

- Shrimp and chicken
- In a bowl, combine smoked paprika, brown sugar, oregano, salt, black pepper, chili powder, cayenne, garlic powder and red crushed peppers.
- Toss chicken thighs and shrimp and add 1 tablespoon olive oil. Rub in thoroughly. Cover and place in refrigerator for 1-2 hours.
- Heat 1 tablespoon in a large skillet. Sear both side of the chicken thighs (about 5 minutes on each side).
- Once golden brown on each side, remove chicken and set aside.
- In the same skillet heat 1 tablespoon of olive oil, cook the shrimp for 1-2 minutes on each side. Remove shrimp and set aside.

Garlic butter sauce
- In a small skillet (you can use the same skillet chicken and shrimp was cook on) melt butter and sauté garlic in for the first 15-30 seconds.
- Add lemon juice and salt to taste.

Garlic mash potatoes
- Bring a large pot of water to a boil. Place potatoes in boiling water, boil for 15-20 minutes or until potatoes are soften.
- Drain water. While hot, mash the potatoes. Add butter, heaving whipping cream, salt, and garlic powder. Mix. (Mixing potatoes with a hand blender for the best results).

LIL SISTER WORD SEARCH

```
B B V V S M F M A Q J Z G P E D A M E M O H C A
C D Q Z V Y P I S C R Z U K V L P Y F C K Y S C
T H P G M Z U S O J J C Z S Z L N T K Z H U W Q
Z N A N Q Q O B Y W M M O F L G X D A Z M B F U
Q C O C Q B J E O I D Y C M V Y K M J M X F S Y
I O A O E R F W D F E V H I X C O I E D N C M S
R C M N E H C T I K S Y G G U P R R T C R H Z A
X A H Z A R G K J G G S S P K Q T E U W S E V G
X T L I J U A U I G K Y K V F I G P C M T F S Q
O L D Y L V X D V O M C X J K V N E H I M R J E
W A R L A I F J O O C K Z T S V R Z H G P L K G
Z N P S T L J C T X J P O Y I A X E J D K E N O
B T W M W A E I U G N K X Y S Z B P V W J J S S
D A L F Q C K K D D S S V T T B P D M H N G F C
T X P I I T R A N W K K H S E E V X M G H C M H
J Z L D O F A O M I J I N N R S T I O R P L P T
H E N K Y D C H F F B L K U S S F K W U P J A U
T A F S E K A C N A P L L W U X X E S B P H S L
C L S T F G J V O W F E K M H V H H V S L A T R
E K Y B R L U P Q X R T Z Q J W J Z J T P C H I
S I P K B T V V C O R N B R E A D Y B T S E A D
O W I X I Y G M M B X C T V N V E V B I F D E R
S G T E C I D N A C D N A I R A M Y N P P T D Y
H I G P F J U E O R X C H Q B X D P J U R E E W
```

CORNBREAD   PITTSBURGH   PUGGYSKITCHEN
ATLANTA   SISTERS   SKILLET   CHEF   RECIPES
HOMEMADE   CHILI   PANCAKES   TIKTOK
SUMMERTIKTOKS   MARIANDCANDICE
CANDICE COOKS

Crab Stuffed Shrimp W/ Lemon Garlic Butter Sauce

INGREDIENT:

STUFFED SHRIMP
1 lb black tiger shrimp
8 oz lump crab meat
½ cup panko breadcrumbs
½ cup onions (finely chopped, sautéed)
3 tbs mayonnaise
1 tbs Dijon mustard
1 green onion(chopped)
½ tsp salt
1 tsp lemon pepper -divided
¼ crushed red pepper
1 tbs olive oil

LEMON GARLIC BUTTER
1 stick unsalted butter
5 tbs olive oil
8 garlic cloves(minced)
1 large lemon juice and zest
salt- to taste

ASPARAGUS
1 lb fresh asparagus – trimmed
1 tbsp olive oil
2 tbs unsalted butter (melted)
2 tbs freshly squeezed lemon juice
½ tsp salt
¼ tsp black pepper

DIRECTIONS:

Crab stuffed shrimp
- Preheat oven to 350 degrees Fahrenheit.
- Peel each shrimp but leave the tail on. Lightly season with ½ tsp lemon pepper and drizzle olive oil. Set aside.
- In a large bowl combine breadcrumbs, onions(sautéed), mayonnaise, Dijon mustard, green onions, salt, ½ tsp lemon pepper, and red crushed peppers. Fold in the crab meat.
- Scoop the crab stuffing into a ball and on to each shrimp with tail facing up, pressing the tail on top (to help secure the stuffing).
- Place in a cast iron pan and bake on 350 degrees Fahrenheit for 10-15 minutes or until cooked.

Lemon Garlic Butter
- In a large skillet, heat butter and olive oil. Stir in minced garlic and sauté for about 30 seconds. Remove from heat.
- Stir in lemon juice and zest. Salt to taste.

Asparagus
- Rinse and trim the ends of the asparagus. Place asparagus on baking sheet. Drizzle olive oil and butter. Add lemon juice, salt,
- and pepper.
- Bake in preheated oven for about 10 minutes or until tender.

Simple Crispy Beer Battered Fish Sandwich

INGREDIENT:

4 cod filets
2 cup flour-divided
1 ½ cup beer
1 tbs creole seasoning
1 tbs garlic powder
½ tbs black pepper
Salt- to taste
Oil- for frying
Brioche buns-for serving

DIRECTIONS:

- Preheat frying oil in a large pot.
- Lightly salt fish on both sides. Set aside.
- On a shallow plate place 1 cup flour.
- In a bowl combine 1 cup flour, creole seasoning, garlic powder, black pepper, and beer.
- Take cod filet, roll in the flour. Then, dip into the beer mixture, and then into the grease.
- Fry for 5-7 minutes or until golden brown and crispy on both sides.
- Serve with tartar sauce and fresh chips or your favorite toppings.

Buttery Foil Wrapped Fish W/ Spinach

INGREDIENT:

1 piece tilapia (or fish of choice)
2 cup spinach(packed)
¼ cup onion (chopped)
2 lemon slices
2 garlic cloves(minced)
5 tbs unsalted butter- divided
¼ tsp garlic powder
¼ tsp smoked paprika
¼ tsp cayenne
¼ tsp salt
Olive oil -drizzled
Foil sheet
3 springs of thyme (or 1 tsp thyme)

DIRECTIONS:

- Preheat oven to 350 degrees Fahrenheit.
- In a small skillet, add 2 tablespoons butter and sauté onions and minced garlic for 3 minutes. Set aside.
- Using a large piece of foil sheet, place packed spinach and 2 tbs of butter.
- Add fish on top of spinach. Seasoning with garlic powder, smoked paprika, cayenne, and salt.
- Drizzle olive oil on top.
- Pour butter and onion mixture on top. Top with lemon slices and thyme.
- Wrap foil tightly, place on baking sheet or pan and bake in oven for 15-18 minutes or until cooked.
- Serve with rice or your favorite side.

Meatball Hoagie

INGREDIENT:

MEATBALL
1 lb 85% lean 15% fat ground beef
1/3 cup onions (finely chopped)
½ cup panko breadcrumbs
3 tbs water
1 tsp garlic paste
1 tsp salt
1 tsp oregano
1 tsp basil
1 tbs olive oil

SAUCE
1 (28oz) can crush tomatoes
1 small onion (sliced)
3 tsp garlic paste
2 tsp oregano
½ tsp salt
2 tsp sugar
1 tsp basil

DIRECTIONS:

- Preheat oven to 400 degrees Fahrenheit.
- In a large bowl, combine ground beef, onions (using food chopper helps get finely chopped), breadcrumbs, water, garlic paste, salt, oregano, basil, and olive oil. Shape mixture into meatballs (ensure each are about the same size).
- Using a sheet pan, place each meatball 1 inch apart.
- Bake uncovered for 20 minutes. Set aside.
- In a large pot add, crush tomatoes, onions, garlic paste, oregano, salt, and sugar. Simmer for 15minutes. Stir occasionally.
- Place meatballs in sauce.
- Add basil and simmer for another 5 minutes. Turn off heat and let sit for 5 minutes before serving.
- Serve with hoagie buns.

Homemade Shrimp Hibachi

INGREDIENT:

Shrimp

1 lb large shrimp
2 tbs unsalted butter
4 garlic cloves(minced)
2 tsp sesame oil
1 tbs soy sauce

Fried rice

2 tbs olive oil
1 cup onion(diced)
1 cup frozen vegetables
2 eggs
2 cup white rice(cooked)
3 tbs soy sauce
3 tbs butter
½ tsp sesame oil

Vegetables

2 tbs olive oil
2 tsp sesame oil
1 onion(sliced)
1 zucchini (sliced)
8 mushrooms(sliced)
1 tbs unsalted butter
1 tbs soy sauce
Salt-to taste

DIRECTIONS:

Fried rice
- In a large skillet, heat olive oil. Add in onions, and vegetables. Sauté until onions are soften.
- Move all vegetables to one side of skillet. Crack both eggs, scramble and fully cook.
- Add rice and butter. Constantly stir in for about 3 minutes.
- Stir in soy sauce and drizzle about ½ tsp sesame oil. Set aside and keep hot.

Shrimp
- Melt butter on low to medium heat, add minced garlic. Sauté for 30 seconds.
- Add shrimp and soy sauce. Cook until shrimp is fully cooked.
- Drizzle sesame oil.

Vegetables
- In another large skillet on medium heat add sesame oil and olive oil.
- Add onions, zucchini, mushrooms, butter, soy sauce, and salt to taste. Sauté until vegetable are tender or until how you like!

Chicken Birria Tacos

Not Authentic, Just My Way!

INGREDIENT:

6 chicken thighs
12 cup water
10 chicken bouillon cubes
Garlic bulb (whole, peeled)
1 large onion (cut in half)
1 large carrot
7 bay leaves
9 guajillo chiles
2 tsp oregano
2 tsp cumin
2 tsp chili powder
To serve
Mozzarella cheese
Corn tortillas
Monterey jack cheese
Cilantro and onions

DIRECTIONS:

- In a large pot, add in water, bouillon, garlic, onion (cut in half), carrot, bay leaves, chiles, oregano, and cumin.
- On medium heat, simmer for 40 minutes.
- Remove chiles, onions and carrots into blender with a few scoops of broth. Blend. Pour mix back in pot.
- Add chicken thighs. Cover with lid and simmer for 1 hour and 30 minutes.
- Stir in chili powder and simmer for another 5 minutes.
- Remove chicken from pot and shred (your thighs should be falling from the bone).
- In a large skillet heat olive oil. Dip tortilla in broth, place on skillet, add chicken and your choice of cheese. Cook each side until golden brown.
- Serve with cilantro and onions!

Spicy Jamaican Beef Patties

Not Authentic, Just My Way!

INGREDIENT:

Filling
1 lb 8% lean 15% fat ground beef
1 tbs avocado oil
1 red bell pepper (finely chopped)
½ cup onions (packed, finely chopped)
2 garlic cloves (minced)
1 tsp salt
1 tsp chili powder
1 tsp garam masala
1 tsp smoked paprika
1 tsp turmeric
½ tsp red chili pepper
½ cayenne powder
1 cup beef broth
1 cup pepper jack cheese(shredded)

Dough
2 cups unbleached flour
2 tsp turmeric
1/2 tsp garam masala
1 tsp salt
5/8 cup vegetable shortening
1/2 water(*cold*)

Egg Wash
1 egg
1 tbs water

DIRECTIONS:

Dough
- In a large bowl mix together flour, turmeric, garam masala, and salt.
- Add in shortening and mix well using your hand until mix looks crumbly.
- Gradually pour water. Mix until dough is formed and roll into a ball.
- Cut dough into 4 pieces and wrap in plastic wrap and refrigerate for 45 minutes.

Filling
- In a large skillet heat avocado oil. Add red pepper and onion. Sauté until onions are soften.
- Add in a chili powder, garam masala, smoked paprika, and turmeric. Toast the seasonings for about 2-3 minutes.
- Add in ground beef. Sprinkle salt and garlic cloves.
- Cook until meat is browned. Once meat is browned sprinkle cayenne and red chili peppers and pour in beef broth.
- Simmer for about 10 minutes, covered. After about 10 minutes a little beef broth should be left and stir in shredded cheese. Set aside to cool.

Egg wash: whisk together egg and water.
- Assemble: PREHEAT OVEN TO 375 DEGREES FARENHEIT. Remove dough from fridge. Sprinkle flour on a flat surface, roll out dough.
- Using a small plate or bowl cut out the outline of the bowl or plate. Scoop a spoonful of filling on to one side of the flat dough.
- Using a little water brush the outer circle of the dough, fold over the dough. Next, using a fork crimp the edges together.
- Place all patties on parchment paper. Brush egg wash on top of each patty. Bake in oven for 20-25 minutes or until done and golden brown/crispy.

Grilled Cheddar-Stuffed Jalapeno Burgers

INGREDIENT:

1 lb (85% lean15% fat) ground beef
1 jalapeno (finely chopped)
1 ½ cup cheddar cheese(shredded)
1 tsp brown sugar
1 ¼ tsp salt
1 tsp black pepper
½ tsp garlic powder
½ tsp dried minced onion
¼ tsp cayenne

DIRECTIONS:

- In a large mixing bowl, add ground beef, jalapeno, brown sugar, salt, pepper, garlic powder, dried minced onions, and cayenne.
- Combine until evenly seasoned.
- Roll into 8 meatballs and press out to make patties.
- Take one patty and place cheese on top. Add another patty on top and press down on the sides to seal cheese. Repeat. Set aside.
- Place patties on preheated and greased grill.
- Grill for about 7-8 minutes on each side or grill burgers to your preference.

Spicy Coated Chicken Sandwiches

INGREDIENT:

4 boneless chicken thighs
1 cup pickle juice
2 cups flour
2 tsp salt
2 tsp pepper
1 ½ tsp cayenne
1 tsp smoked paprika
1 cup buttermilk
1 egg
2 tbs hot sauce

Oil Coating
1/4 tsp red crushes peppers
1/2 cup frying oil
2 tbs unsalted butter
1 tbs brown sugar
2 tsp cayenne
1/2 tsp chili powder
1/2 tsp smoked paprika
1/2 tsp garlic powder

DIRECTIONS:

- Start by marinating your chicken. Place chicken thighs and pickle juice in a large bowl. Marinate for 1 hour. (The longer you marinate, the better)!
- Whisk together buttermilk, egg and hot sauce Set aside.
- In another bowl mix flour, salt, pepper, cayenne, and paprika. Mix well.
- Make oil coating. Mix all ingredients listed above. Set aside
- Dip chicken into flour, and then dip into buttermilk mixture, then back into the flour. Make sure each piece of chicken is coated evenly.
- Let coated chicken sit out for 10-15 minutes.
- Fry each piece of chicken until fully cooked and golden brown on each side.
- Pour and coat each chicken with oil coating.
- Serve.

(Puggys) Personal Seafood Bag W/ Spicy Onion Sauce

INGREDIENT:

Crab boil bag

2 crab clusters
½ lb. large shrimp
4 red potatoes (boiled)
1 corn (cut & boiled)
Beef smoked sausage(sliced)
2 eggs (boiled)
1 lb crawfish
2 sticks butter (melted)
Medium-sized oven bags
1 ¼ tsp creole seasoning 2 slices of onions
1 tbs garlic herb
1 tsp smoked paprika
1 tsp garlic powder
1 tsp cayenne

Spicy onion sauce

1 stick unsalted butter
Hot sauce(splash)
Worcestershire sauce(splash)
¾ tsp creole seasoning
¼ tsp smoked paprika
¼ tsp chili powder
¼ tsp cayenne
½ tsp garlic cloves (minced)
¼ tsp red crushed pepper

DIRECTIONS:

- Preheat oven to 350 degrees Fahrenheit.
- Place oven bag on a sheet pan, add shrimp, potatoes, corn, sausage, crawfish, and crab clusters. (Place each in the order listed).
- Sprinkle creole, garlic herb, paprika, garlic powder, and cayenne.
- Pour melted butter evenly over seafood.
- Close bag lightly. (Do not tie bag!) Bake in oven for 25 minutes or until shrimp are cooked.
- Add boiled eggs and serve.

Spicy onion sauce

- In a small skillet heat butter and 2 slices of onions (JUST SLICES, NOT WHOLE ONIONS).
- Add 2 splash of hot sauce, 2 splashes of Worcestershire sauce. Simmer for 1 minute
- Sprinkle seasonings. Simmer for 2 minutes.
- Add garlic and stir in for 30 seconds. Remove from heat. Serve.

Shrimp Alfredo

INGREDIENT:

PASTA SAUCE
Angel hair pasta- (cooked, drained)
3 cups heavy whipping cream
2 sticks unsalted butter
1 tsp salt
1 tsp pepper
4 tsp garlic(minced)
4 cups parmesan cheese

SHRIMP
18-20 large shrimp
1 stick unsalted butter
2 tsp garlic herb
½ tsp creole seasoning
1 tsp cayenne
1 tsp smoked paprika
1 tsp garlic powder
2 tsp minced garlic

DIRECTIONS:

Shrimp
- Melt butter in large skillet.
- Add shrimp. Sprinkle garlic herb, creole, cayenne, paprika, and garlic powder and minced garlic.
- Stir in for 2-4 minutes or until shrimp is fully cooked.
- Remove from heat. Set aside.

Pasta Sauce
- In a large pan, add butter and heavy whipping cream. Simmer for 1- 2 minutes.
- Whisk in garlic, salt, and pepper for 1 minute.
- Whisk in parmesan cheese until blended.
- Add angel hair noodles Top shrimp mixture. Serve.

Creamy Spaghetti Bake

INGREDIENT:

12 oz spaghetti noodles (cooked)
1 lb 85% lean 15% fat ground beef(cooked/drained)
1 ½ cup cheddar cheese(shredded)
¼ cup water
¼ cup parmesan cheese
½ cup green peppers(diced)
1 cup onions(diced)
(4 oz) can mushrooms(undrained)
3 tbs olive oil
14.5 oz diced tomatoes(undrained)
1 (2 ¼ oz) can olives(drained)
2 tsp oregano
2 tsp salt
½ tsp black pepper
2 tsp basil
2 garlic cloves(minced)
Can of cream of mushroom
1 ½ cup Monterey jack cheese(shredded)

DIRECTIONS:

- Preheat oven to 350 degrees Fahrenheit.
- Heat olive oil in a medium pot. Add ground beef, salt, pepper, oregano, and basil. Stir occasionally for 5 minutes.
- Add bell peppers and onions, stir until tender.
- Add diced tomatoes, mushrooms(undrained), and garlic cloves. Stir occasionally for 10 minutes uncovered.
- In a separate pot pour in ¼ cup water, cream of mushroom, and parmesan. Stir until well blended. Set aside.
- Using baking dish, follow these steps. First place half of spaghetti noodles down, ground beef mixture, shredded cheese, more spaghetti noodle, ground beef mix, shredded cheese. Now, you want to pour the creamy mix on top.
- Bake(uncovered) for 30-45 minutes. Serve.

Shrimp Mac

INGREDIENT:

4 cup corkscrew noodles- (cooked and drained)
3 cups heavy whipping cream
4 tbs butter
1 cup parmesan cheese
2 cups Monterey jack cheese
2 tsp garlic herb
2 cups mozzarella cheese(shredded)

SHRIMP
10-15 shrimp
1 tbs olive oil
Salt – to taste
Pepper – to taste
Garlic powder – to taste
Smoked paprika – to taste

DIRECTIONS:

- Start by making sauce. In a small pot, melt butter and pour in heavy whipping cream.
- Stir in parmesan, Monterey cheese, and garlic herb.
- Add noodles in sauce. Fold until combined.
- Pour mac into desired baking dish.
- Top with mozzarella. Bake for 20-25 minutes.
- In a small bowl add shrimp. Sprinkle salt, pepper, garlic, and paprika.
- Drizzle olive oil in a small skillet and add shrimp. Cook until done.
- Top Mac with shrimp. Serve.

Deviled Eggs

INGREDIENT:

6 eggs
2 tbs mayonnaise
1 tsp honey mustard
4 tsp relish
½ tsp black pepper
¼ tsp salt
1 tsp sugar
1 green onion(optional)
Shrimp or bacon(optional)

DIRECTIONS:

- Place eggs carefully into cold water with 1 tbs salt (the salt helps the shell peel off easily).
- Simmer for about 9 minutes. Remove from heat and drain water. Fill pot with cold water and peel eggs.
- Cut the eggs in half (lengthwise).
- Remove yolk and place in a small bowl.
- Add mayonnaise, honey mustard, relish, black pepper, salt, sugar, and green onions. Mash up with a fork until well blended.
- Fill egg whites with yellow filling. Serve with your favorite toppings.

Stovetop Candied Yams

INGREDIENT:

4 sweet potatoes
8 tbs unsalted butter
1 cup brown sugar
1 tbs vanilla extract
½ tsp salt
1 tsp cinnamon
½ cup white sugar

DIRECTIONS:

- Scrub, peel and cut sweet potatoes (try to cut ½ inch round) set aside.
- In a medium pan, on medium heat melt butter and combine brown sugar, white sugar, salt, cinnamon.
- Add in sweet potatoes and stir in until fully covered. Simmer for 10 minutes.
- Remove lid and reduce mixture on low heat for about 15 minutes or until potatoes are tender.
- Stir in vanilla and serve.

Nette's Collard & Kale Greens

INGREDIENT:

2 bunch collard greens
2 bunch kales
1 onion(diced)
½ cup olive oil
1 whole jalapeno(chopped)
3 tbs smoked paprika
8 bouillon cubes
11 cups of water
Smoked turkey leg(optional)

DIRECTIONS:

- Wash and rinse collard greens and kale thoroughly. Drain and cut the stems. Chop greens and kale.
- In a large pot heat olive oil on medium heat. Add onions and jalapenos. Sauté until tender.
- Stir smoked paprika for about 1-2 minutes. Add bouillon cubes and pour the water in. Add in smoked turkey. (optional).
- Place both collard greens and kale into pot.
- Cook on medium to high heat for about 2 hours or until tender. Stir occasionally and if the pot liquid is getting low, add ½ cup water at a time.

Potato Salad

INGREDIENT:

2 large yellow potatoes
8 eggs-(boiled)- divided
2 tsp salt
2 tbs sugar
1 tsp pepper
3 heaping tbs relish
2 tbs honey mustard
2 celery sticks (finely chopped)
3 green onions(chopped)
1 cup mayo

DIRECTIONS:

- Place potatoes to a small pot of cold water and bring to a boil. Boil for 20minutes (or until easily poke with a knife). Drain and set aside.
- Cool for 10 minutes or until cool to handle. (The potatoes should still be warm)
- Peel skin on each potato and cut into small cubes.
- In a large bowl, add potatoes. Gently fold in salt, pepper, and sugar.
- Gently fold in relish, honey mustard, mayo, celery, green onions and 6 eggs(diced).
- Top with the rest of the sliced eggs. Serve.

Lasagna Roll-Ups

INGREDIENT:

1 lb ground beef
1 bell pepper(chopped)
6 garlic cloves(minced)
1 onion(chopped)
3 tbsp olive oil
4 cups water
2 (6oz) tomato paste
3 tsp oregano
1 tsp basil
4 tsp salt-divided
½ tsp black pepper
1 tsp sugar
1 8oz block mozzarella cheese(shredded)
Pack of Lasagna noodles- (cooked, drained)

Filling

16 oz ricotta
1 cup parmesan cheese
4 tsp oregano

DIRECTIONS:

- In a small bowl mix together ricotta, oregano, and parmesan (use filing ingredients listed above). Set aside.
- In a large pot, add olive oil on medium heat. Add ground beef, 2 tsp salt, and oregano. Stir in for 5 minutes, chopping beef up.
- Add onions, bell peppers, and garlic into the pot. Stir occasionally until veggies are tender.
- Add tomato paste, water, 2 tsp salt, sugar, basil, and black pepper. Stir occasionally, let sauce simmer on medium for 20 minutes.
- Using a lasagna noodle spread ricotta mixture and sauce. Repeat for each noodle.
- Roll up the noodle and place on a baking pan.
- Pour remaining sauce and shredded cheese on top. Cover and bake for 20-25 minutes. Serve

Creamy Vegetable Pasta

INGREDIENT:

1 ½ cup Rotini pasta noodles (cooked, drained)
2 tbs unsalted butter
2 tbs all-purpose flour
2 cups half and half
2 chicken bouillon cubes
½ tsp salt
¼ tsp pepper
1 tbs olive oil
2 tbs minced garlic
2 ½ cups frozen mixed vegetables
½ tsp thyme
½ tsp oregano
¼ tsp red crushed peppers(optional)
¼ cup parmesan cheese

DIRECTIONS:

- In a medium saucepan heat butter. Whisk in flour for about 2 minutes.
- Add half and half, bouillon cubes, salt, and pepper. Whisk until smooth and sauce is a bit thicken.
- Remove from heat and set aside.
- In another pot on low to medium heat, add olive oil and minced garlic. Stir in for 30 seconds.
- Add frozen veggies. Sprinkle thyme, oregano, and crushed red peppers.
- Pour veggie mixture into saucepan.
- Add rotini noodles.
- Stir in parmesan cheese. Serve.

The Best Mac and Cheese Recipe

INGREDIENT:

3 cup elbow noodles
8 tbs unsalted butter
¼ cup onions (finely chopped)
(12 oz) evaporated milk
Can of cream of chicken
(2 oz) cream cheese(cubed)
(8oz) Sharp cheddar block (shredded)
(8oz) Monterey jack block (shredded)
(16oz) Velveeta cheese block(cubed)
1 tbs garlic herb seasoning

DIRECTIONS:

- Boil elbow noodles (salt the water), drain.
- Preheat to 350 degrees Fahrenheit.
- Start by making cheese sauce. In a large pot, melt butter and add onions. Sauté until onions are soften. Add milk, Velveeta, cream of chicken, and cream cheese. Whisk until cheese is melted. Set aside.
- Place elbow noodles in pan. Spread both shredded cheeses and garlic herb on top.
- Pour cheese mixture on top. Stir in well.
- Place in oven and bake, covered for 15 minutes.
- Stir and leave uncovered. Bake for another 20 minutes.

Twice Baked Potatoes

INGREDIENT:

2 large russet potatoes
1 cup Monterey jack(shredded)
1 cup sharp cheddar(shredded)
3 tbs butter
2 green onions
½ cup sour cream
¼ cup heavy whipping cream
¼ tsp pepper
1 tsp salt
¼ tsp onion salt
Olive oil
Chives-optional
Cheddar cheese-for topping

DIRECTIONS:

- Preheat oven to 350 degrees Fahrenheit.
- Scrub potatoes clean. Pat dry. Rub potatoes with olive oil. Bake potatoes for about 1 hour and 30 minutes or until potatoes are done
- (Soft inside and crisp on the skin).
- Remove from oven and let sit for 10 minutes. (Do not let potatoes set longer than 10 minutes, potatoes must be warm!)
- Cut potatoes lengthwise. Scoop the insides into a mixing bowl (leave a layer of the potato insides to keep the potatoes skin from tearing).
- Add shredded cheeses, butter, salt, pepper, onion salt, heavy whipping cream, sour cream. Mix (using hand mixer).
- Stir in green onions.
- Fill each potato skin with the filling.
- Place on baking sheet or pan, top with shredded cheese and chives.
- Bake for 20-25 minutes. Serve.

Blackeye Peas W/ Okra & Cornbread

INGREDIENT:

Blackeye Peas
2(15.5oz) can blackeye peas-drained and rinsed
2 cup okra (sliced)
1 onion(diced)
4 tbs olive oil
2 celery hearts (finely chopped)
6 cups water
8 bouillon cubes
1 tsp cayenne
2 tbs smoked paprika

Cornbread
1 cup cornmeal
1 cup flour
2/3 cup sugar
1 tbs baking powder
¼ tsp salt
1 cup milk
2 eggs
1 unsalted stick butter(melted)
Honey-to top
2tbs butter-to top

DIRECTIONS:

Blackeye Peas
- In a small pot, add oil olive. Add in onions and celery. Sauté until onions and celery are soften.
- Add In blackeye peas, water, bouillon cubes.
- Sprinkle cayenne and paprika.
- Simmer on low to medium heat for about 20 minutes.
- Add fresh okra. Simmer for about 10 minutes.
- Remove from heat and serve.

Cornbread
- Preheat oven to 350 degrees Fahrenheit.
- Spray baking pan or (rub butter and coat with flour evenly).
- In a large bowl, combine corn meal, flour, sugar, baking powder, and salt.
- In another bowl mix egg, milk, and butter.
- Combine dry and wet ingredients together.
- Pour mix into baking pan. Bake for about 25 minutes.
- Once corn bread is done and out the oven place 2 tbs butter and a squeeze of honey and spread. Serve.

Garlic Green Beans

INGREDIENT:

(16oz) bag green beans
½ cup onions (finely chopped)
3 tbs olive oil
2 tsp salt
4 garlic cloves-(minced)

DIRECTIONS:

- Heat olive oil in a large skillet.
- Add onions and green beans. Sauté for 7 minutes.
- Add in salt and garlic. Stir in for about 30 seconds.
- Remove from heat and serve.

Pot Roast

INGREDIENT:

3 lb chuck roast
1 large onion(sliced)
2 celery sticks(chopped)
3 garlic cloves(minced)
½ lb baby carrots
2 cups water
5 chicken bouillon cubes
1 tsp basil
1 tsp oregano
½ tsp salt
Olive oil-drizzle

DIRECTIONS:

- Preheat oven to 350 degrees Fahrenheit.
- Rinse and pat dry roast.
- Salt both sides of roast. (To taste) Drizzle one side of roast with olive oil.
- Place roast in preheat skillet, with oiled side down. Drizzle oil on the other side facing up.
- Sear both side of meat, 6 minutes on each side.
- Remove roast from pan. Set aside in roasting pot.
- In the same skillet add water, scrape the bottom. (If the pan bottom is too burnt, skip this step, and add water in roasting pot)
- Using a roasting pot, add your meat, water from pan, onion, celery, garlic, carrots, bouillon, basil, oregano, and salt.
- Cook for about 2 ½ -3 hours. Occasionally checking and spooning the juice over the meat.
- Let meat rest for 5-10 minutes. Serve.

Broccoli Cheese Soup

INGREDIENT:

3 cup water
4 bouillon cubes
4 cups fresh broccoli(chopped)
1 celery stick(chopped)
1 carrot stick(shredded)
1 cup onion(chopped)
¼ cup flour
4 cup sharp cheddar(shredded)
2 cups heavy whipping cream
5 tbs butter
1 tsp minced garlic
½ cup sour cream

DIRECTIONS:

- In a small pot, bring 3 cups water to a boil. Add bouillon cubes, carrots, and celery. Simmer on medium heat for 5-8 minutes.
- Then, add your broccoli. Simmer until soften. Set aside until completely cooled. (Room temperature).
- In another pot, on low heat add butter and onions. Sauté until onions are soften.
- Add garlic. Sauté for 1 minute.
- Whisk in flour for 3-5 minutes.
- Whisk in heavy whipping cream(gradually).
- Stir in broccoli mixture (pour in whole pot with the broth), shredded cheese, and sour cream. Simmer for about 5 minutes or until hot.
- Serve with crackers or in bread bowl.

Sweet Potato Pie

INGREDIENT:

1 (29 oz) can of yams
4 tbs unsalted butter(melted)
(4 oz) cream cheese (room temperature)
1 ½ tsp vanilla extract
1 ½ tsp cinnamon
¼ cup evaporated milk
½ cup sugar
1 deep dish pie crust
2 eggs (room temperature)

DIRECTIONS:

- Preheat oven to 350 degrees Fahrenheit.
- In a large mixing bowl, add yams, butter, cream cheese, vanilla, cinnamon, milk, sugar, and eggs. Mix, blend well (I recommend hand mixer).
- Pour mix in the deep-dish pie crust.
- Bake pie for 45-50 minutes.

Fish Tacos W/ Slaw & Crispy Jalapenos

INGREDIENT:

4 cod filets
2 cup flour-divided
1 ½ cup beer
1 tbs creole seasoning
1 tbs garlic powder
½ tbs black pepper
Salt- to taste
To serve
2 avocados (sliced)
Crispy jalapenos
Corn or flour tortillas

Slaw
(9oz bag) Shredded green and red cabbage
1/2 cup mayo
1/2 tsp garlic powder
1/2 tsp salt
1/2 tsp pepper
1 lime (juiced)
1/4 cup cilantro *(chopped)*
1 green onion *(chopped)*

DIRECTIONS:

Fried cod
- Preheat frying oil in a large pot.
- Cut cod into strips. Lightly salt fish on both sides. Set aside.
- On a shallow plate, place 1 cup flour.
- In a bowl combine, 1 cup flour, creole seasoning, garlic powder, black pepper, and beer.
- Take cod pieces, roll in the flour. Then, dip into the beer mixture and then into the grease.
- Fry for 5-7 minutes or until golden brown and crispy on both sides.

Slaw
- In a small bowl, whisk together mayo, lime juice, garlic, salt, and pepper.
- In another bowl, combine shredded cabbage, cilantro, and green onions.
- Toss in mayo mixture. Refrigerate for about 30 minutes (optional but recommended).

Assemble: Using a corn or flour tortilla, heat all of them on a large skillet with a drizzle of olive oil. Once you are done heating tortillas, add fish, slaw, avocado, and crispy jalapenos. Serve.

Blt Salad

INGREDIENT:

16 oz penne noodles (boiled, drained, rinsed)
1 pack bacon(cooked)
1 cup sour cream
1 cup mayo
1 pack hidden valley ranch seasoning packet
6 -8 green onions(chopped)
1 romaine lettuce heart(chopped)
16 oz grape tomatoes(sliced)

DIRECTIONS:

- In a large bowl, whisk mayo, sour cream, and ranch packet.
- Stir in penne noodles (make sure noodles are at room temperature).
- Add green onions, lettuce, tomatoes.
- Crumble the bacon and stir in.
- Refrigerate for about 1 hour. Serve.

Easy Pierogi

Not Authentic, Just My Way!

INGREDIENT:

Dough
4 cups flour
1 cup water
2 eggs
1 ½ tsp salt

Potato Filling
3 medium yellow potatoes
2 cups sharp cheddar(shredded)
½ cup sour cream
¼ cup ricotta cheese
½ cup onion (finely chopped)
2 tsp salt
½ tsp onion salt
½ tsp pepper
3 tbs butter

DIRECTIONS:

Dough
- Place flour in a large bowl. Add water, eggs, and salt. Using your hand, mix well to form dough.
- Using a flat surface, add sprinkles of flour and knead the dough until smooth for about 5-8 minutes.
- Cut dough into 4 pieces.
- Wrap each with plastic and allow dough to rest for 30-40 minutes.

Potato filling
- In a small skillet add butter and onion. Sauté until onions are soften. Set aside.
- Peel and cut potatoes (into 4 medium size cubes).
- Place potatoes in cold water and bring to a boil. Boil for 15-20 minutes or until potatoes are done (should be easily poked with a fork).
- Mash and Let chill for 10 minutes.
- Add cheese, sour cream, ricotta, sauté onions, salt, onion salt, and pepper.

To assemble: Sprinkle flour on the surface. Using a rolling pin, roll dough 1/8 inch thick. Cut out circles (using a 3-inch cookie cutter or a glass cup). Using about a tablespoon of filling, roll into a ball. Place filling into the dough and fold the dough over to seal the filing and pinch the edges closed.

To cook: Bring a large pot of salted water to a boil. Add pierogies. Boil until each float to the top. Remove and set aside. Heat 4 tbs butter in skillet and cook for 5 minutes. Serve with sauteed onions and sauerkraut. If you like crispy pierogies add some olive oil to skillet!

Easy Pepper Steak & Rice

INGREDIENT:

1 lb flank steak(sliced)
½ tsp onion salt
½ tsp pepper
1 tbs ginger
6 garlic cloves(minced)
1 cup chicken broth
3 tbs olive oil
Rice-of your choice
1 bell pepper(sliced)
Half of large onion(sliced)
1 cup low sodium soy sauce
3 tsp cornstarch
¼ tsp red crushed peppers
2 tbs brown sugar

DIRECTIONS:

- In a small bowl, mix soy sauce and cornstarch. Set aside.
- In a large bowl, add steak. Sprinkle onion salt and pepper.
- On medium heat, add olive oil and steak to a large skillet. Cook until steak is browned.
- Stir in garlic and ginger for 2 minutes.
- Pour in chicken broth and cornstarch mixture. Simmer for about 5-6 minutes (the sauce should be a little bit thicker).
- Add bell peppers, onions, red crushed peppers, and brown sugar. Simmer for another 5-8 minutes.
- Serve with rice.

Easy Chicken Pot Pie

INGREDIENT:

2 chicken thighs (cooked & shredded)
2 cups chicken broth
8 tbs unsalted butter
1 yellow onion (finely chopped)
6 tbs all-purpose flour
2 cups evaporated milk
2 cups frozen mixed vegetables
1 tsp salt
½ tsp black pepper
1 tsp ground sage
1 tsp thyme
(16.3 oz) Jumbo flaky biscuits

DIRECTIONS:

- Preheat oven to 325 degrees
- In a large pan, heat butter and onions. Sauté until onions are soften. Whisk in flour for about 3 minutes.
- Pour in milk. Whisk until thicken. Sprinkle in salt, pepper, sage, and thyme.
- Pour in chicken broth. Whisk until mixture is smooth.
- Add cooked shredded chicken and frozen vegetables.
- Place biscuits on top.

(If you are using a cast iron keep the mixture in same pan, if not remove into proper baking pan before placing biscuits on top).

- Rub butter on top of biscuits (this step is optional).
- Bake for 20-25 minutes.

Ms. Lady's Favorite

INGREDIENT:

30-35 medium shrimp (deveined, peeled, steamed)
¼ cup purple onion (finely chopped)
1 celery stick (finely chopped)
¼ cup mayonnaise
1 tbs Dijon mustard
¼ tsp lemon juice
¼ tsp salt
¼ tsp pepper

DIRECTIONS:

- In a large bowl, whisk together mayo, mustard, and lemon juice.
- Toss the steamed shrimp (room temperature), onions, and celery. Stir until combined.
- Season with salt and pepper. Refrigerate.

Cream Shrimp Spinach Artichoke Dip

INGREDIENT:

4 cup fresh spinach(chopped)
(8oz) cream cheese(softened)
1 tbs olive oil
¼ cup onions (finely chopped)
8-10 large shrimp (peeled and deveined)
2 tbs unsalted butter
1 tsp creole seasoning
(12oz) jar of artichoke hearts (drained and chopped)
¼ cup mayonnaise
¼ cup sour cream
2/3 cup parmesan cheese
1 cup Monterey jack cheese(shredded)
1 cup mozzarella cheese(shredded)

DIRECTIONS:

- Preheat oven to 350 degrees Fahrenheit.
- Using a small skillet add olive oil and onions. Sauté for 1 minute. Add butter, shrimp, and creole seasoning and cook until lightly pink
(Do not cook fully)! Remove from heat and set aside.
- In a large bowl add in spinach, cream cheese, artichoke, mayo, sour cream, parmesan, and Monterey jack. Stir until fully combined.
- Add shrimp and onions into the bowl with spinach mixture. Stir until combined.
- Evenly Pour mixture into a proper baking pan. Place In oven.
- After about 15 minutes in the oven, stir dip and add mozzarella on top. Bake for another 10 minutes.
- Serve with tortilla or pita chips!

BEGINNER COOK TIP/SUGGESTIONS:

Clean as you go- As a cook you should never let a mess pile up.
Time your food properly- If you are preparing a meal be sure to know what to start cooking first. To ensure everything is hot at the same time!
Never use damp or wet oven mitts- you will burn yourself!
Always rinse your rice- It removes all the excess starch.
Always salt your pasta and rice water!
Don't overcrowd pan- you want everything to cook evenly and brown!
Let meat rest before slicing-if you cut before resting the meat, you will lose some flavor juices and meat will become tough!
Let meat sit out before frying- makes meat juicer and ensure temperature doesn't drop when placed on heat!
Keep a piece of ginger in freezer- easier to shred!
Store onions in plastic bag/refrigerate-prevents them from drying out!
Wrap paper towel in with green onions after opening- prevent them going bad fast!
After opening bag of spinach, place paper towel on the side of the bag -keeps them fresh longer, the paper towel helps absorb moisture.
Once you cut tomato, place on paper towel-absorbs moisture, prevent mushy tomatoes.
Store your tomatoes on counter- prevents mushy tomatoes/ going bad fast.
Store asparagus in the fridge in a cup of water- keeps asparagus from going bad fast.
Read the whole recipe before cooking- prevents mistakes while cooking!
Don't leave the kitchen- this is important, some recipes can be easily burned, or you can lose track of time!
After cutting green onions, place stems in a cup of distilled water- they will continue to grow.

Hamburger Steak & Gravy

INGREDIENT:

1 lb (85% lean 15% fat) ground beef
3 tbs breadcrumbs
½ cup onion (finely chopped)
1 large onion (sliced)
1 ½ cup of beef broth
2 tbs all-purpose flour
2 tbs olive oil
4 tbs unsalted butter
6 mushrooms (sliced)
1 tsp garlic powder
½ tsp smoked paprika
1 ½ tsp salt (divided)
1 tsp Worcestershire sauce
1 tsp fresh thyme

DIRECTIONS:

- Combine ground beef, breadcrumbs, finely chopped onions, garlic powder, paprika, and 1 tsp salt. Form 4 patties into thick circles.
- Heat olive in a large skillet. Add patties and cook until both sides have a little crisp.
- Remove patties from pan and set aside.
- In the same skillet, melt butter.
- Add sliced onions and mushrooms and cook for about 4 minutes.
- Sprinkle flour over the mushrooms and onions. Stir.
- Whisk in beef broth.
- Add Worcestershire sauce, fresh thyme and ½ tsp salt. Add patties back into pan
- Simmer for 8-10 minutes. Serve.

Simple Tomato Soup

INGREDIENT:

2 (28oz) can San Marzano tomatoes
6 tbs butter
3 cups yellow onion(chopped)
6 garlic cloves(minced)
1/3 cup flour
4 cups chicken broth
4 basil sprigs
¼ cup parmesan cheese
1 tsp sugar
Salt-to taste

DIRECTIONS:

- In a large pot on medium heat, melt butter and add onions. Sauté until onions are soften.
- Add garlic. Sauté for 30 seconds. Whisk in flour, stir for about 2 minutes.
- Gradually pour in chicken broth. Whisk until fully blended.
- Place cans of tomatoes, parmesan, sugar, basil, and your preference of salt.
- Simmer for about 20-25 minutes. Thoroughly stir occasionally until tomatoes are soften and falling apart.
- Remove from heat and into the blender. (If you use hand blender, you can keep mix in pot). Blend until smooth.
- Serve.

Fried Shrimp W/Buffalo Sauce

INGREDIENT:

1 lb large shrimp (peeled, deveined)
Frying oil
1 tsp lemon pepper
Dry
1 cup all-purpose flour
¼ cup cornstarch
1 tsp salt
¼ tsp smoked paprika
½ tsp garlic powder
¼ tsp cayenne

Wet
1 egg
1 tsp hot sauce
¼ cup milk

Dipping Sauce
2 tbs butter
¼ cup ketchup
¼ cup hot sauce

DIRECTIONS:

- Rinse shrimp with cold water and pat dry. In a large bowl with shrimp sprinkle lemon pepper.
- On a shallow plate, mix all dry ingredients together until combined.
- In a small bowl, whisk in all wet ingredients.
- Preheat frying oil on medium heat.
- Coat the shrimp in the flour mix, then into the egg mixture, and back into flour mixture. (Coat shrimp well with flour and make sure to shake excess flour off!)
- Gently place the coated shrimp into preheated oil.
- Fry for 5 minutes or until golden brown.

Dipping Sauce
- In a small saucepan, heat butter. Add ketchup and hot sauce. Simmer for about 2 minutes. Remove from heat and dip or drizzle over shrimp.

Lazy Beef Stroganoff

INGREDIENT:

2 cups of wide egg noodles (cooked and drained)
1 lb ground beef
12 crackers- (crushed)
5 garlic cloves(minced)
6 sprigs thyme
2 sprig rosemary (divided)-chopped
1 small onion (finely chopped)
Salt-to taste
Pepper- to taste
2 tbs Olive oil
2 cups chicken broth(divided)
2 packs pioneer brown gravy
2 cups water
1 onion (sliced)
1 bell pepper(chopped)
½ tsp onion salt
8 mushrooms(sliced)
1 cup sour cream

DIRECTIONS:

- In a large bowl combine ground beef, crushed crackers, garlic, thyme, 1 rosemary sprig, finely chopped onions, and 2 tbs of chicken broth.
- Add salt and pepper to taste. Shape mixture into meatball shape (ensure each are the same size).
- In a large mixing bowl whisk together the 2 cups water and both gravy packets. (Make sure you stir thoroughly to ensure no powder is left inside bowl). Set aside.
- In a large pan heat olive oil. Add meatballs. And cook for 3 minutes on each side or until meatball are done.
- Add in the rest of the chicken broth, gravy mixture, bell peppers and onions. Simmer on low heat for 15 minutes, the mix should thicken up.
- Stir in 1 rosemary sprig, onion salt, and mushrooms. Simmer for another 5 minutes.
- Add sour cream. Simmer for 5 minutes. Serve over wide egg noodles.

Chicken Tikka Masala
Not Authentic, Just My Way!

INGREDIENT:

Chicken Marinate
3 boneless chicken thighs (cut, cubed)
1 cup plain yogurt
3 garlic cloves(minced)
1 ½ tsp ginger(minced)
2 tsp garam masala
½ tsp salt
Half of lemon(squeezed)
Optional
1 Onion(sliced)
1 Bell peppers(sliced)

Tikka Masala Sauce
2 tbs olive oil(divided)
2 tbs ghee
1 cup onions(diced)
4 garlic cloves(minced)
1 tbs ginger (minced)
2 tsp coriander
2 tsp garam masala
1 tsp cumin
1 tsp turmeric
1 tsp chili powder
2 cups tomato sauce
1 cup coconut milk

DIRECTIONS:

- In a large bowl combine all chicken marinate ingredients together. Marinate for 3 -6 hours (the longer you marinate the better)!
- In a large saucepan add 1 tbs olive oil. Add chicken and cook for about 10 minutes (ensure that you cook for 5 minutes on each side).
- Remove chicken from the pan. Set aside.
- In the same skillet add ghee and 1 tbs olive oil. Add onion. Sauté until soften.
- Add garlic clove and ginger. Sauté for 1 minute.
- Sprinkle coriander, cumin, turmeric, chili powder, and gram masala. On low heat, Toast in the spices for about 2-3 minutes.
- Pour in tomato sauce and coconut milk. Simmer for about 10 minutes.
- Add in bell peppers, onions, and chicken. Simmer for another 10 minutes.
- Serve with rice and naan.

Vanilla Cake Crusted Cherry Cheesecake

INGREDIENT:

1 box vanilla or yellow cake
4 eggs
2 tbs olive oil
2 (8 oz) cream cheese packages (room temperature)
½ cup sugar
1 ½ cup Half and half
3 tbs lemon juice
1 tbs vanilla
(21 oz) can cherry or strawberry filling

DIRECTIONS:

- Preheat oven on 325 degrees.
- Open the cake mix and set aside 1 cup.
- In a large mixing bowl combine in the rest of the cake mix, 1 egg, and 2 tbs olive oil. Mix thoroughly.
- Using a 9x13 cake pan, press the mix in the bottom and side. Set aside.
- Blend together the cream cheese and sugar. Add the remaining eggs and the 1 cup of cake mix. Using hand mixer mix for about 1-2 minutes.
- In another bowl, Combine milk, lemon juice, and vanilla. Mix until well blended. Gradually blend into cream cheese mixture for about 2-3 minutes.
- Pour mix on top of cake crust.
- Bake for 40-55 minutes.
- Remove from the oven and let cool.
- Top with filling. Refrigerate.

Tan Tan Men Ramen

Not Authentic, Just My Way!

INGREDIENT:
2 green onions-chopped
2 eggs
2 Bok choy-steam or boiled
(9.5oz) Pack of Japanese ramen noodles

Tare (Seasoning sauce)
3 tbs tsuyu (soup base)
2 tbs tahini
1 tbs chili oil

Soup
1 cup water
2 cups unsweetened soy milk
4 bouillon cubes

Meat
½ lb ground beef
3 tbs chili oil
1 tbs garlic-minced
1 tbs ginger-shredded
1 tbs chili bean paste
1 tbs oyster sauce
Sweet cooking rice wine-drizzle

DIRECTIONS:

- Start by boiling ramen noodles (salt the water) and egg (Boil the perfect egg for about 6 minutes in boiling water). Set aside once done.
- In a small bowl, make your tare. Mix Tsuyu, tahini, and chili oil. Set aside.
- In a large pot, make your soup. Add water, soy milk and bouillon cubes.
- Simmer for about 8 minutes on low heat. After 8 minutes, remove from heat.
- In a small skillet add all meat ingredients together. Cook and ground up meat until fully cooked and browned.
- Drizzle rice wine on top of browned meat and set aside.
- Mix the tare and soup together.
- Pour soup mix in bowl, add ramen, Bok choy, ground beef mixture, eggs, and green onions. (FOLLW THESE STEPS IN ORDER TO PLATE)! Serve.

Spicy Creole Jambalaya

INGREDIENT:

2 tbs olive oil-divided
1 pack (12 oz) beef smoked sausage
2 bell pepper-diced
1 onion-diced
1 celery stick-diced
6 garlic cloves-minced
1 lb crawfish
3 tsp creole seasoning
½ tbs thyme
3 tbs unsalted butter
½ tsp oregano
1 ½ tsp red crushed peppers
½ cayenne powder
2 ¾ chicken broth
1 (14oz) can crushed tomatoes
1 ½ cup long grain rice
1 lb large shrimp
1 green onions-chopped

DIRECTIONS:

- In a large pan on medium heat drizzle 1 tablespoon olive oil. Add smoked sausage. Cook for 3 minutes. Remove from pan. Set aside.
- In the same pan drizzle another tablespoon of olive oil. Add in bell pepper, onions, and celery. Sauté until veggies are soften.
- Sprinkle in minced garlic, creole seasoning, thyme, oregano, red crushed pepper, and cayenne. Stir in for about 1 minute.
- Stir in chicken broth, rice, and crushed tomatoes. Cover with lid. Constantly stir and Simmer for about 35 minutes.
- In a separate skillet heat 3 tbs butter and sauté shrimp for about 4 minutes.
- Steam your crawfish for about 8 minutes.
- Once the rice is about done, add shrimp and sausage back in the pan. Continue to cook for about 5 minutes.
- Remove from heat. Serve with steamed crawfish and top with green onions.

Chessy Beefy Skillet

INGREDIENT:

1 lb ground beef (85% lean 15% fat)
2 tbs olive oil-divided
8oz Velveeta block cheese
½ cup onions(diced)
1 bell pepper(diced)
1 tbs ketchup
1 tbs Dijon mustard
2 tbs taco seasoning(divided)
1 ½ cup elbow noodles(uncooked)
3 ½ cup chicken broth
2 cup cheddar cheese(shredded)

DIRECTIONS:

- In a large skillet, heat 1 tablespoon olive oil. Add ground beef. Cook until ground beef is fully cooked and browned. Drain grease.
- In the same skillet drizzle 1 tablespoon olive oil. Stir in onions and bell peppers. Sauté for about 3-5 minutes.
- Turn heat down to low heat and add in ketchup, mustard, 1 tablespoon of taco seasoning, elbow noodles, broth, and Velveeta cheese. Stir until combined.
- Simmer for about 20 minutes covered, Stirring occasionally. (Until noodles are cooked fully)!
- Stir in shredded cheese and sprinkle 1 tbs taco seasoning.
- Simmer for another 5 minutes.
- Remove from heat. Serve.

Strawberry Cupcakes Topped W/ Vanilla Frosting & Funnel Cakes

INGREDIENT:

Cupcakes
1 (15.25oz) yellow cake mix
½ (3.4oz) vanilla pudding mix
1 ½ stick butter(softened)
½ cup water
4 eggs
2 tsp vanilla extract
10-12 strawberries-diced

Frosting
2 sticks salted butter(softened)
3 cups powdered sugar
3 tbs heavy whipping cream
1 ½ tsp vanilla extract

Funnel cake
1 cup buttermilk pancake mix
1 ½ sugar
1 tsp vanilla extract
½ cup water

DIRECTIONS:

- Preheat oven to 350 degrees Fahrenheit. Place cupcake liner in cupcake pan, or grease cupcake pan.
- In a large mixing bowl, with a hand mixer beat together cake mix, pudding mix, butter, water, eggs, and vanilla.
- Beat for about 1-2 minutes or until well blended. Stir in strawberries.
- Evenly scoop batter into cupcake pan.
- Bake for about 20 minutes or until the tops bounce back when lightly touched. Set aside to chill.

Frosting
- In a mixing bowl with a hand mixer beat the butter until creamy and smooth.
- Gradually add the powdered sugar on medium speed (make sure mix is well blended before the next step).
- Add heavy whipping cream, a tablespoon at a time. Beat for another few seconds. Stir in vanilla extract.

Funnel Cake
- Preheat a pot with frying oil.
- In a bowl, add pancake mix, water, sugar, and vanilla.
- Pour batter into a small zip loc bag, cut a tiny hole at the tip of the bag.
- Drizzle batter in mini circles, creating mini funnel cakes!

Assemble: When cupcakes are completely cool. Pipe the icing on each cupcake, add your mini funnel cakes and half of strawberries.

You can drizzle with some strawberry syrup (totally optional)!

Salmon Patties

INGREDIENT:

2 (14.75oz) can salmon (drained, remove any bones if any)
1 egg
¼ cup mayo
1 cup onion (finely chopped)
2 greens onions
½ tsp salt
½ tsp lemon pepper
½ cup panko breadcrumbs

DIRECTIONS:

- In a bowl combine salmon, (make sure that no bones are in mix, remove all bones) egg, mayo, onions, green onions, seasonings, and breadcrumbs.
- Form patties. Chill for about 20-30 minutes in refrigerator.
- Heat olive oil in a large skillet. (Do not fill oil, make sure oil is shallow in the skillet).
- Cook patties until browned on both sides or for about 3 minutes on each side. Serve.

Stuffed Peppers

INGREDIENT:

6 large bell peppers
1 lb (85% lean 15% fat) ground beef
½ cup short grain rice(steamed)-make sure you salt your water
2 tbs olive oil
1 small yellow onion(diced)
2 garlic cloves(minced)
1 (14.5oz) can Italian style diced tomatoes (w/basil, garlic, oregano)
2 tbs tomato paste
1 tsp dried oregano
½ tsp salt
½ tsp black pepper
1 cup mozzarella cheese(shredded)

DIRECTIONS:
- Preheat oven to 350 degrees Fahrenheit.
- Rinse and pat dry bell peppers. Cut bell peppers in half or cut the top and remove the insides and the seeds.
- In a large pot, on medium heat add olive oil. Add ground beef, onions, oregano, garlic, salt, pepper. Cook until beef is fully browned.
- Stir in tomato paste and diced tomato can. Simmer for about 5 minutes.
- Add in steamed rice. (Make sure you salted your rice water)!
- Scoop the ground beef mixture into each pepper and place your choice of shredded cheese on top.
- Bake for about 15 minutes, covered with aluminum foil.
- Uncovered for 10 minutes or until pepper are soften.

Simple Creamy Tomato Pasta

INGREDIENT:

16oz cooked pasta- your choice
5 garlic cloves-minced
4 tbs butter
2(14 fl oz) can tomato sauce
4 tbs tomato paste
1 ½ cup heavy whipping cream
½ tsp thyme
½ tsp oregano
Salt- to taste
Parmesan cheese

DIRECTIONS:

- In a large skillet melt butter. Add garlic and sauté for about 1 minute.
- Stir in tomato paste, tomato sauce, heavy whipping cream, thyme, and oregano. Simmer for about 8 minutes. (The sauce should be a little thickened),
- Add in your preference of salt and parmesan cheese.
- Stir in cooked pasta, Serve.

Baked Fish W/ Cilantro Topper

INGREDIENT:

BAKED FISH
2 lb. Robalo whole *fish (clean, gutted)*
Creole seasoning- *to taste*
Cayenne- *to taste*
Oil-*drizzle*
1 lemon- *sliced*

CILANTRO TOPPER
1 bunch cilantro
1 lime- *(peeled, sliced)*
2 garlic cloves
½ cup olive oil
Red crushed peppers - *to taste*
Salt -*to taste*

DIRECTIONS:

BAKED FISH
- Preheat oven to 350 degrees Fahrenheit.
- Rinse and pat dry fish.
- Cut 3 slits into the side of the fish.
- Season with creole seasoning and cayenne pepper, the inside and out.
- Drizzle whole fish with olive oil.
- Tuck lemon slices into the slits and the inside of fish.
- Bake for 45-55 minutes or until fish is fully cooked.

CILANTRO TOPPER
- Using a blender, place all ingredients above.

Serve with rice.

Creole Shrimp Etouffee

INGREDIENT:

Broth
Scraps from onions and celery
2 cups water
2 bouillon cubes
shrimp shells
half of lemon-*sliced*

Sauce
4 tbs unsalted butter
4 tbs unbleached all-purpose flour
1 ½ cup onion-*diced*
½ cup celery-*diced*
½ cup bell pepper-*diced*
4 garlic cloves-*minced*
1 *(14 oz)* can diced tomatoes
1 tsp thyme
1 tbs creole seasoning
3 splashes of hot sauce

Shrimp
14-20 large shrimp *(deveined, peeled)*
½ tsp creole seasoning

DIRECTIONS:

Cut and prep everything before the following steps. (Do Not throw away scraps!)

BROTH
- Place all the ingredients listed above in a small pot. Simmer on low heat for about 20 minutes. Strain scraps from broth and set aside.

SAUCE
- Melt butter in a large pan until brown. Whisk in flour for about 10 minutes until the roux turns dark brown. Add in celery, peppers, and onion Sauté until soften for about 10 minutes.
- Add in garlic and thyme Saute for 1-2 minutes. Whisk in broth.
- Add tomatoes and creole seasoning, hot sauce and salt to taste. Simmer for about 15 minutes.

SHRIMP
- Season with creole seasoning.
- In a small pan over medium heat drizzle olive oil and add shrimp. Sauté until shrimp is fully done.
- Serve with rice!

General Tso Chicken

INGREDIENT:

CHICKEN
1 lb chicken boneless chicken breast (sliced, cubed)
½ tsp garlic powder
1 tsp salt
½ tsp smoked paprika
½ tsp onion powder
2 eggs
1 cup unbleached all-purpose flour
cooking oil

SAUCE
3 tbs sweet cooking rice wine or rice vinegar
3 tbs soy sauce
2 tsp hoisin sauce
1/4 cup water
3 tbs sugar
1 tbs cornstarch
1 tbs minced ginger
1/2 tsp red chili flakes
2 garlic cloves *(minced)*
sesame seeds *(optional)*

DIRECTIONS:

CHICKEN
- Preheat cooking oil in a large pot.
- Place chicken in a bowl. Sprinkle seasonings listed above.
- In a separate bowl whisk egg. Set aside.
- Place flour in a separate bowl.
- Dip chicken in flour mixture, then egg mixture and then back in flour.
- Fry each piece of chicken for about 3-5 minutes or until golden brown and cooked.
- Remove and set aside.

SAUCE
- In a small bowl whisk together rice wine, soy sauce, hoisin sauce, water, sugar, and cornstarch.
- In a large saucepan drizzle olive oil. Add red chili flakes, garlic cloves, and ginger. Suate for about 30 seconds. Add in mixture that you set aside.
- Toss in chicken and cook for another 1 minute or until sauce is thickened.

Made in the USA
Monee, IL
22 May 2025

bfa03664-9ef5-4f7c-add2-eee07ce80e4eR01